HOPE

COMFORT AND ENCOURAGEMENT
FROM THE **BIBLE**

By Bruce Bickel & Stan Jantz

Bob Siemon Designs • Santa Ana, California

Published by: Bob Siemon Designs
                             3501 W. Segerstrom Ave.
                             Santa Ana, CA 92704
                             1-800-854-8358
                             www.bobsiemon.com

ISBN: 0-9659733-6-0   Printed in the U.S.A.

CONTENTS

INTRODUCTION

If ever there were a need for hope, it is now. Most people today are facing uncertainties they haven't experienced in their lifetimes. The economic crisis alone is creating extraordinary stress. For several months now the news has been filled with reports about staggering losses on Wall Street and plummeting home prices, which have combined to wipe out the retirement savings of millions. Many companies that were thriving just a short time ago are now declaring bankruptcy or dramatically downsizing, swelling the ranks of the unemployed. As a result, many people are anxious and fearful. They are wondering, what kind of future are we facing?

As if the economy were not enough to cause anxiety and fear, we all must face the ongoing challenges of everyday life. Some of us are experiencing health issues, while others are dealing with friends or family members who are fighting a life-threatening disease. Many of us are confronted with the pressures of broken relationships, while others are weighed down by global concerns. When you take all of these things into account, it seems as though the whole world is groaning.

If ever there were a need for hope, it is now. That's why we are offering you this book of hope, filled with comfort and encouragement from the Bible. In these troubled times, we need more than human opinion and human solutions. We need God's perspective and God's help, which He offers through the Bible, His written word:

> *"For I know the plans I have for you," declares the LORD, "plans to prosper you and not to harm you, plans to give you hope and a future."*

Jeremiah 29:11

God's plans for us are always the best, and they are usually part of a journey from where we are to where God wants us to be, and from who we are now to who God wants us to be in the future. In other words, God wants to change us even as we are experiencing change. He wants us to change from people who are weak and fearful into people who have strength and courage. He wants us to practice integrity and develop perseverance.

As you read this book, may the words of the Bible comfort and encourage your heart. And may it fill you with hope as you share hope with others.

—Bruce & Stan

CHANGE

...put off your old self, which is being corrupted by its deceitful desires...put on the new self, created to be like God in true righteousness and holiness.

Eph. 4:22-24

CHANGE

Change is never easy. Even when your life is going relatively well, change can be challenging. At the heart of change is the notion of something becoming different than it was, but during good times you don't see that as a negative. In fact, you may even initiate change: you get a new job, you move to a new city, you buy a house, you get married, have kids, those sorts of things.

However, in troubled times, when things aren't so good—you lose your job, lose your home, go through a rough patch in your marriage, have a falling out with one of your kids, find out that someone you love has cancer, those sorts of things—change can be devastating. In fact, it's the act of change itself—passing from one place, state, form, or phase to another—that is the most stressful.

If that's the case for you, then right now you and just about everybody else on this planet are stressed to the max. Because right now our world is undergoing the greatest change in recorded history. You think that's an exaggeration? Consider the evidence:

• Our world is going through the greatest *technology change* ever. The ways we communicate with one another, receive information, view entertainment, get treated medically, and perform everyday tasks are changing at breakneck speed. Technology is good, technology is necessary, but when it comes at you like a fire hose, it can be completely unnerving and put you under tremendous stress.

• Our world is going through the greatest *moral change* in history. You used to be able to count on people to behave within the bounds of certain universal moral guidelines. A person's word was his or her bond. People told the truth. There were socially accepted practices that were decent and mutually respectful. Not these days. Today immoral behavior has permeated the very institutions we have always counted on: our banks, our schools, our government, even our churches. It doesn't seem as though you can trust anybody anymore. This is a huge change from the way things used to be, and it's causing a lot of stress.

• No doubt the greatest change you are currently going through is *economic change*. Even if your own financial situation is fairly secure (and that's a big *if*), you are likely feeling the pressure of the catastrophic economic fallout going on all around you. And if you are a victim of the global economic meltdown, you are probably going through the greatest stress of your life. Like millions of people, you may have lost big money in places you thought would make you money, or at the very least keep you secure: your paycheck, your stock portfolio, your 401k, and especially your house. In a matter of months, much of your security has disappeared. Talk about stress!

How Are You Feeling Now?

The changes we have been discussing so far didn't happen overnight. The changes in technology, morality, and the economy have been years in the making. What makes them so dramatic and stressful is that everything is changing all at once. It's like we're experiencing a perfect storm of change. As a result, the change seems abrupt and especially brutal.

When you consider the seemingly random change that can strike at any instant—an accident, a devastating storm, an act of violence, or a disease—you begin to wonder what in the world is going on and how in the world will you be able to cope. We recently received an e-mail from someone who just discovered something horrible about a loved one:

> *My dad has recently been diagnosed with cancer. I don't understand why! He has always done everything for anyone. He doesn't have an enemy in the world. No one. And now God is making him sick. This is not fair! He is my dad! I didn't have a close relationship with God before this, but now I find myself doubting everything. I am very bitter towards God.*

Clearly this person is expressing emotions common to anyone faced with extraordinary and seemingly senseless change. There are feelings of helplessness, anger, doubt, resentment, blame, and most intensely, fear.

Fear is the most primal of all human emotions, and fear is at the heart of change. Fear is what makes change so difficult. Fear is what makes change so difficult, because nobody wants to be afraid. But change is unavoidable, even in good times. Now, as we go through some really hard times, change is almost unbearable, mainly because we're all very much afraid.

How long can we go on like this? Well, we can endure the current climate of change for a while, but none of us can handle such a high level of stress—induced by change and fear—forever. At some point things will start to break down. Since none of us knows how long this current environment of change will last, we desperately need to find a way to deal with it. And because it's impossible to find a way *out* of the current climate, we need to find a way *through*.

There Is a Way Through

If you're like most people, you're doing your best to find a way through the current storm. You are looking for some kind of certainty in this time of change. The changes all around are just too great. The fear is too intense. You need hope.

Where do you go to find hope?

For hundreds of years people have turned to the Bible for help and for hope. The Bible isn't just another book filled with wise sayings and ancient history. The Bible is literally the word of God, written by real flesh-and-blood people inspired by God to deliver His message of love and hope to all of humanity—and that includes you, right here, right now. Even though the Bible was written long ago, its message reaches out across the centuries to where you are.

All Scripture is inspired by God and is useful to teach us what is true and to make us realize what is wrong in our lives. It corrects us when we are wrong and teaches us to do what is right. God uses it to prepare and equip his people to do every good work.

2 Timothy 3:16,17, NLT

The Bible has a lot to say about change and fear. Mostly, the Bible tells us to have no fear. In fact, the most common admonition in the Bible is, *"Do not be afraid."* We see it again and again, mostly through the people in the Bible who—just like you—were going through difficulties brought about by circumstances beyond their control.

Abraham is one of the most famous people in the Bible. He's a central person in three religions: Christianity, Judaism, and Islam. When Abraham was asked by God to leave his homeland and travel a great distance to a place he didn't know, he was fearful. Even though God was asking him to change, it didn't erase the fear in his heart or make it any easier. He was going into the great unknown, where he would be a stranger in a strange land. Abraham was fearful, so he turned to God in faith, asking Him for assurance during a time of great uncertainty. God told Abraham:

"Do not be afraid...I am your shield and your very great reward."

Genesis 15:1

David, who wrote most of the Psalms, is another famous figure in the Bible. As a child, David was a shepherd and he learned the importance of protecting his sheep from being attacked by their predators. When David became king over a great nation, he was the one being attacked by his enemies, so he turned to God as his Great Shepherd for protection, guidance, hope, and comfort.

Even though I walk through the valley of the shadow of death, I will fear no evil, for you are with me; your rod and your staff, they comfort me.

Psalm 23:4

Peter, one of the twelve disciples of Jesus, often experienced times of doubt and uncertainty. Once he was with his friends in a boat being rocked by the wind and waves. It was late and it was dark. Then, Peter and the others saw Jesus in the distance, walking on the water towards them. Not wanting to wait any longer for Jesus to reach them, Peter got out of the boat and walked on the water towards the Lord. But when he took his eyes off Jesus and focused on the storm around him, he began to sink and became very afraid. Immediately, Jesus reached out his hand, caught Peter, and said:

"You of little faith...why did you doubt?"

Matthew 14:31

How Will You Respond?

What about you? Are you like Peter, wanting to trust the Lord, but so focused on the storm around you that you are sinking? You need to take your eyes off the storm and have faith in God. As Jesus told Peter, fear comes when you doubt God's ability to get you through the storm. Faith is trusting in the one true God, who is greater than all and can be trusted in all situations.

Are you like David, going through a deep, dark valley? It's natural to worry about your life and fear the future, but focusing on your own worries and fears won't help you. If you've lost all hope, rather than blaming God, it's time to turn to God, who longs to comfort you with His light and strength.

The LORD is my light and my salvation—
whom shall I fear?
The LORD is the stronghold of my life—
of whom shall I be afraid?

Psalm 27:1

Are you like Abraham, going through a time of great change? Are you fearful of an unknown future? You don't need to be afraid. God is speaking to you right now, telling you to trust Him by faith. You don't know what the future holds, but God does. He will be with you no matter where you go.

That's not to say that you won't have troubles. God never promised us a life free from difficulties. But what He does offer is a way *through* the difficulties, *through* the valleys, *through* the storm, *through* the change.

Jesus knows what it's like to go through difficulties, valleys, and storms because He personally experienced all of them. He knows what it's like to go through stressful times of change. That's why He can tell us, *"Do not be afraid."*

"Peace I leave with you; my peace I give you. I do not give to you as the world gives. Do not let your hearts be troubled and do not be afraid."

John 14:27

Tell God, "Here I am"

We hope you have been encouraged by these words of comfort from the Bible. But we need to tell you that just reading them isn't enough. God wants to help you, but he needs something from you. He needs you to tell Him, *"Here I am."* Those simple words speak volumes to our awesome God. They are the words Abraham said when faced with a huge trial. He was willing to obey God. When you say to God, *"Here I am,"* you are telling Him that you are willing to do anything He asks of you.

And what is God asking you to do? Most of all, He is asking you to trust Him and to be willing to change—but it's not the kind of change you have to fear. This kind of change is all about transformation, where you give up your self-centeredness and self-focus and allow God to change you from the inside. This kind of change is all about becoming the kind of person God wants you to be.

...put off your old self, which is being corrupted by its deceitful desires; to be made new in the attitude of your minds; and to put on the new self, created to be like God in true righteousness and holiness.

Ephesians 4:22-24

God cares deeply about what you're going through, but He cares even more about the person you're becoming. As you continue to read this book, you're going to discover ways God wants to change you, even as you experience change. And in the midst of that change, there is hope.

STRENGTH

I have learned the secret of being content in any and every situation, whether well fed or hungry, whether living in plenty or in want. I can do everything through him who gives me strength. Phil. 4:12-13

STRENGTH

How strong are you feeling right now? We're not talking about your *external*, physical strength. That depends mainly on your genetics and your conditioning. No, the kind of strength we're referring to is *internal* and involves your mind, your will, your heart, and your soul. It's the kind of strength that gives you mental toughness, inner resolve, confidence, and peace.

So we'll ask you again: *How strong are you feeling right now?* If you're like most people who have been rocked by all the change in today's world, you may not be feeling strong at all. And if you are facing some adversity (and who isn't these days?), you may be feeling mentally drained, your inner resolve may be non-existent, your confidence could be low, and your heart could be somewhat troubled.

Does any of this sound familiar? Of course it does. You've been in adverse situations before, so you know the feeling. Maybe you had a demanding and unreasonable boss who made life miserable for you, or you were faced with a deadline that seemed impossible to meet. Maybe you went through a period of time when you had trouble paying your bills, or you were struggling in a relationship. You've faced adversity before, but somehow you found the strength to overcome it.

This time, however, it seems different. You aren't just dealing with a demanding boss; you've lost your job. You aren't just having trouble paying your bills; you've lost your home. You aren't just struggling in a relationship; something very serious is going on.

With adversity mounting you may be feeling especially weak and helpless. You've forgotten what it feels like to have strength, and you're wondering what you can do to get it back. What are you going to do? Well, before we can talk about strength, we have to deal with adversity, because the two are inextricably linked.

The Truth About Adversity

It's unrealistic to think we deserve a life free from troubles and adversity, yet that's what many people have come to expect. Even those who believe in God grow weak in the knees and lose their confidence when bad things happen. Sometimes they even blame God for their problems because they believe a loving God would never allow His children to suffer.

The truth about adversity is this: *It happens to everyone.* No one escapes, not even those who put their trust in God. If anything, those who follow Jesus Christ should be more prepared for adversity than anyone else because Jesus guaranteed that we would have trouble. At the same time, He wants His followers to know something very important. When faced with adversity, when staring trouble in the face, you can find strength in Him. Jesus says,

"I have told you these things, so that in me you may have peace. In this world you will have trouble. But take heart! I have overcome the world."

John 16:33

Isn't that amazing? Jesus Christ, who is God in human form, came to earth to live a perfect life as an example for us, and then overcame the greatest adversity of all so that we could have peace and confidence in the midst of our own adversity. The truth is, God never promised to deliver us *from* adversity, but He has promised to deliver us *in* adversity. When you come to understand that, you will come to understand one of the great truths of life.

Where Real Strength Comes From

Not only do we incorrectly think that God wants to keep us from adversity, but we also wrongly conclude that we have the strength to get through our troubled times. Moses, who is known in history as the great deliverer—he's the one who led the Israelites out of Egypt and slavery—learned that his strength was not enough to get the job done.

If anyone was qualified to be a strong man, it was Moses. Raised as a Prince of Egypt in the house of Pharaoh, the ruler of Egypt, Moses had the best training and the finest teachers. For the first 40 years of his life, he was on top of the world. Then he hit a wall of adversity and had to flee to the desert, away from his position and power. For another 40 years Moses lived a quiet, unassuming life in the wilderness.

That's when God met him in the form of a burning bush (see the third chapter of Genesis). When Moses stopped to look at this amazing sight, God called to him: *"Moses, Moses."* Do you know what Moses said in reply? *"Here I am."* Do these words sound familiar? They should. That's what Abraham said when God called to him. Those are the words God wants to hear from us. When we say to God, *"Here I am,"* we are acknowledging our need and telling Him we are available.

God told Moses He had a big task for him: He wanted Moses to lead His people, the Israelites, out of Egypt. Suddenly this man who was once very strong felt incredibly weak. He objected to God's assignment, complaining that he lacked the ability to carry out this seemingly impossible request. He told God, "Who am I that I should go to Pharaoh and bring the Israelites out of Egypt?" (Exodus 3:11).

Moses lacked confidence and credibility. Instead of focusing on God's strength, he was obsessed with his own weakness. But God was patient with Moses and assured him that He would be the one delivering His people. All Moses had to do was trust and obey.

As soon as Moses took his eyes off his own weakness and focused on God's strength, God used him to deliver His people out of Egypt and across the Red Sea against the mightiest army on earth.

And when the Israelites saw the great power the LORD displayed against the Egyptians, the people feared the LORD and put their trust in him and in Moses his servant.

Exodus 14:31

The people understood that it was not the strength of Moses that accomplished the impossible. It was God's strength working through a willing person. Moses also recognized this unique principle—that God's strength is displayed through weak but willing people—when he composed this song immediately after the great victory:

The LORD is my strength and my song;
he has become my salvation.
He is my God, and I will praise him,
my father's God, and I will exalt him.

Exodus 15:2

Where is your strength coming from? If you think you are strong enough to get through the adversity you are facing right now, you may be facing an uphill battle. If you are willing to trust God and obey Him, He will be your strength and your salvation. That's what He did for Moses, and He promises to do the same for you.

In fact, God is actively looking for people who are willing to trust and obey Him. He isn't looking for people who put their trust in their own strength and self-sufficiency. God is looking for people who realize they are unable to walk through the valley alone, who recognize they aren't strong enough to overcome the adversity they are facing, and who realize they aren't strong enough to do what God is asking them to do.

For the eyes of the LORD range throughout the earth to strengthen those whose hearts are fully committed to him.

2 Chronicles 16:9

Weakness Comes Before Strength

There's a verse in the Bible that says, *"Pride goes...before a fall"* (Proverbs 16:18). You don't have to look very far to see how often this principle is illustrated in our world. Consider all of the "captains of industry" and people with great wealth and power who have fallen from the pinnacles of prosperity and position to the lowest places. What happened to them? They may have been proud and arrogant people who believed they were exempt from adversity, yet it was their pride that brought them down.

The apostle Paul, the great missionary who did more to spread the good news about Jesus than anyone else except for Jesus himself, was once a proud, arrogant person. In the first century as the church was just beginning, Paul was a great religious leader who led the persecution against those who professed faith in Jesus Christ. The Bible says he *"began to destroy the church. Going from house to house, he dragged off men and women and put them in prison"* (Acts 8:3). Paul was the epitome of a proud, strong man.

Then God literally knocked him off his horse and called out to him: *"Why do you persecute me?"* (Acts 9:4). In an instant Paul knew that he needed to trust God and obey Him. And so he began a new life of following Jesus and building up the church rather than destroying it. Paul paid a dear price for this dramatic turn of events. The powerful people he once helped now turned against him, putting him in prison and beating him many times. Whereas he once was powerful and strong, Paul became vulnerable and weak, experiencing unusual adversity. *"I have labored and toiled and have often gone without sleep,"* Paul wrote. *"I have known hunger and thirst and have often gone without food"* (2 Corinthians 11:27).

What kinds of adversity are you experiencing right now? There is nothing you are going through that great leaders like Moses and Paul have not gone through before. These were people who loved God and were willing to serve Him. When God asked them to do something that seemed impossible, they simply said, *"Here I am."* When faced with adversity, rather than drawing upon their own strength, they acknowledged their weakness. They knew the *"upside down"* principle that God wants to teach you:

When you are weak, then you are strong.

This principle runs so contrary to the way the world operates, that it almost seems foolish. But if you trust God in the middle of your adversity, you're going to find the truth and the beauty of that powerful phrase. Here's the way Paul put it:

But he said to me, "My grace is sufficient for you, for my power is made perfect in weakness." Therefore I will boast all the more gladly about my weakness, so that Christ's power may rest on me. That is why, for Christ's sake, I delight in weaknesses, in insults, in hardships, in persecutions, in difficulties. For when I am weak, then I am strong.

2 Corinthians 12:9-10

God Will Renew Your Strength

Just because you admit your weakness doesn't mean that you won't be strong. Weakness does not equal meekness. Some of the strongest leaders in the world today are the most humble because they depend on God for their strength. They recognize that God is almighty and all-powerful, yet He cares for each of us personally and desires to strengthen us for the challenges we face each day.

God knows that even the strongest people get weary. Even the most optimistic among us gets discouraged. It's during those times of weariness and distress that we need to acknowledge God as our source of strength. When you feel that you can't go another step, when you come to the point where life is crushing you beneath its cares and concerns, remember that you can call upon God to help you and renew your strength.

The LORD is the everlasting God, the Creator of the ends of the earth. He will not grow tired or weary...He gives strength to the weary and increases the power of the weak. Even youths grow tired and weary, and young men stumble and fall; but those who hope in the LORD will renew their strength. They will soar on wings like eagles; they will run and not grow weary, they will walk and not be faint.

Isaiah 40:28-31

When you realize that God is looking for those whose hearts are fully committed to Him, so that He may strengthen them; when you understand that God's strength will come to you in your weakness; when you believe that God will renew your strength when you grow weary; and when you depend on God for your effectiveness rather than your own effort and talent, you will come to know what it means to have hope. Because only then will you understand where your help comes from.

Put your faith in God by asking Him to give you strength, and God will be true to His word. He will give you the strength you need to get through any situation, resulting in true contentment no matter what your circumstances are.

I know what it is to be in need, and I know what it is to have plenty. I have learned the secret of being content in any and every situation, whether well fed or hungry, whether living in plenty or in want. I can do everything through him who gives me strength.

Philippians 4:12-13

COURAGE

Be strong and courageous. Do not be terrified; do not be discouraged, for the LORD your God will be with you wherever you go.

Joshua 1:9

COURAGE

In the last chapter we talked about strength, which is the power to do something. God has promised to give us strength when we need it, and His strength works best in our weakness. As long as we take pride in our self-sufficiency, we will miss out on God's sufficiency. You see, God is the perfect gentleman. He won't force Himself on us. But He will provide the strength we need when we admit our weakness and ask for His power.

Strength is an essential quality when we are faced with adversity. But strength alone won't get us through adverse situations, whether short-lived or long-term. We also need courage, which by definition is *"the quality of mind or spirit that enables a person to face danger, difficulty, or pain without fear."*

Be Strong and Courageous

In the Bible the words *strong* and *courageous* are often used together. The first time we see this is towards the end of Moses' life. Realizing that he is about to die, Moses gathers the people of Israel together to give them his final words of instruction and encouragement. Here's what he says:

"Be strong and courageous. Do not be afraid or terrified...for the Lord your God goes with you; he will never leave you nor forsake you."

Deuteronomy 31:6

Even though he led God's people out of Egypt, Moses knew that he was not going to lead them into the Promised Land. You would think that Moses had everything needed to get the job done. The Bible says, *"And it was through Moses that the Lord demonstrated his mighty power"* (Deuteronomy 34:12). Moses was a leader with great strength of mind and spirit, but it required more than power and strength to lead the Israelites to their ultimate goal. God needed a leader with extraordinary courage.

That leader was Joshua, who was Moses' second in command, and one of the finest examples of courage in the entire Bible. When Moses sent 12 spies on a reconnaissance mission behind enemy lines to see if it was possible to occupy the Promised Land, ten of the spies said it was too dangerous. Only two of the spies—Joshua and Caleb— said it could be done. Because Joshua demonstrated courage, Moses chose—and God confirmed—Joshua to be his successor.

After the death of Moses, Joshua assumed command, and God immediately began to give His new leader a set of instructions. Here's what God said to Joshua:

"Be strong and courageous. Do not be terrified; do not be discouraged, for the LORD your God will be with you wherever you go."

Joshua 1:9

The similarity in the language of the verses in Deuteronomy and Joshua is no coincidence. God values courage, which is the motivation to do what needs to be done, whether it's overcoming adversity or taking on a challenging task. And there's no question that God desires to provide courage for those whose hearts are fully committed to Him. He longs to help us and He promises to be with us wherever we go, as long as we invite Him into the details of our lives.

Courage is the motivation to do what needs to be done, whether it's overcoming adversity or taking on a challenging task.

Include God in Your Plans

Joshua was courageous and successful because he carefully obeyed God's commands every step of the way (you can read all about Joshua in the book of the Bible that bears his name). Whether he was faced with incredible obstacles or was confronted with his enemies, Joshua included God in his plans.

Have you ever noticed how God has a way of upsetting our plans when we don't include Him? It's so easy to get caught up in our own plans, especially in the practical, everyday issues of life, and then we act surprised when things don't go exactly the way we want them to go. Very often, that's because we've left God out of our planning. It's okay to make plans—in fact, God wants you to plan. But He also wants to be included in your plans, no matter how small.

The Lord directs the steps of the godly. He delights in every detail of their lives.

Psalm 37:23, NLT

Why wouldn't we want to draw upon God's wisdom in everything we do? Why wouldn't we want to invite the Creator of the universe, who knows us better than anyone, who has our best interest in mind always, and who knows the future when we don't, to be involved in everything we do? Even if the best we can do is to move forward, we can move forward with courage because we know that God is with us in every detail of our lives. Here's what God is saying to you right now:

"I will never fail you. I will never abandon you." So we can say with confidence, "The LORD is my helper, I will have no fear. What can mere people do to me?"

Hebrews 13:5-6, NLT

These are powerful words! This isn't some person telling you, *"I will never fail you."* This is almighty God, who is bigger than your fears, yet so close to you that he knows every detail of your life. Are you facing financial uncertainty? Are you in the middle of a difficult illness or a troubled relationship? God is aware of your physical and emotional troubles. Trust in God to give you the courage you need to get through.

When it seems as though there is nothing and no one to help you, tell yourself, *"The Lord is my helper."* Put your trust in God's assurance and then with courage, say out loud, *"I will have no fear!"* Realizing how frail and helpless you are doesn't mean you are a coward. Just the opposite is true. Those who say, *"The Lord is my helper"* are courageous, for they recognize where their courage comes from.

It Takes Courage to Move Forward

Sometimes you need courage to do something significant. But most of the time you need courage just to move forward. Sometimes it takes courage just to get out of bed in the morning and face the day. Do you ever feel that way? If that's the case, then for you, courage may need to be measured in small steps—and that's okay.

God delights in every detail of your life, so taking even small steps forward is a demonstration of great courage. Being willing to accept change and set some new goals shows God that you have courage. You can move forward without fear, and you can change into a new person even as the world around you is changing, as long as you remember that God is with you wherever you go. Here again are the words God gave to Joshua:

"Be strong and courageous. Do not be terrified; do not be discouraged, for the Lord your God will be with you wherever you go."

Joshua 1:9

INTEGRITY

Guard my life and rescue me; let me not be put to shame, for I take refuge in you. May integrity and uprightness protect me, because my hope is in you.
Psalm 52:20-21

INTEGRITY

Usually when we think about God, especially when we are hurting or when we are in trouble, we think about how God can help us. That's good! God likes it when we call on Him for help. The Bible tells us, *"God is our refuge and strength, an ever-present help in trouble"* (Psalm 46:1). God loves to give us things, just like a father loves to give things to his children. But just like an earthly father loves it when his children give him things, our heavenly Father loves it when we give things to Him.

On the surface, this may seem like an unreasonable request. What can we humans—weak and frail and prone to make mistakes—give to our perfect, all-powerful God who has everything? The answer may surprise you, because it isn't anything tangible, like money.

Neither is the gift intangible, like your time. That's not to say that God doesn't want you to handle your money and time in the right way, but what He wants more than anything else is *you*. More precisely, the most important thing you can give God, and the thing He desires most from you, is your integrity.

The Gift of Integrity

What is integrity, and why does God value it so highly? In a word, *integrity* is all about who you are on the inside. Integrity is the inner quality of the heart that shapes your character. Integrity is what happens in your life when no one's looking.

Everyone else values who you are on the outside—the way you look, how you act, what you say. But God most highly values who you are on the inside.

"The LORD does not look at the things man looks at. Man looks at the outward appearance, but the LORD looks at the heart."

1 Samuel 16:7

When God looks at your heart, what does He see? If He sees a heart that's whole and wholly devoted to Him, He will see a heart of integrity. That's because *wholeness* is at the heart of integrity. When you have integrity, it means you have complete honesty. You can be trusted to do the right thing in all situations.

If an object (such as a bridge or a building) or a person (such as you) has integrity, it means the object or the person is in an unbroken condition. If a bridge lacks integrity, it means there are some broken places in the structure, and it can't be trusted. Likewise, if your life lacks integrity, you can't be trusted. Oh, you may fool people on the outside, just like a bridge can give off the appearance of being perfectly sound. But if there are broken places in your character, you can be sure God knows.

The Titanic, once considered the greatest ship ever built, is a great illustration of what happens when integrity breaks down. One of the primary reasons people thought the Titanic was unsinkable was because of the compartments built into its hull. The theory was that flooding in one compartment due to a breach (that's a broken place) in the hull wouldn't affect other compartments because of the high walls between them. What the Titanic's designers did not anticipate was that the fateful collision with the iceberg slashed through several compartments at once, so that the seawater spilled over the walls from one compartment to another until the mighty ship tragically sank.

The same principle applies to your life. You think you can keep a break in one part of your life from impacting the other parts, but it just doesn't work that way. A breach of integrity in one compartment of your life quickly spills over to another until your entire life begins to sink. You think your honesty in one part of your life, the part that people see, will cover for the dishonesty in another part of your life, the part that people don't see. But it doesn't work that way. When you're dishonest in one area, your entire life is affected.

As the business guru Tom Peters once observed, "There's no such thing as a minor lapse of integrity."

When Your Integrity Breaks

Sometimes when you feel like your life is sinking, it's because of circumstances beyond your control. This is the time you can tell God, *"Here I am"* as you call upon Him for strength and courage. Other times, when you feel like your life is sinking, it's because of your choices or your decisions. Often, it's because your integrity has been compromised.

Such was the case with King David, one of the great leaders in the Bible. David was the founder of Jerusalem, an ancestor of Jesus, and a person God referred to as *"a man after my own heart"* (Acts 13:22). At the height of his powers, David made some terrible choices that affected other people in profound ways. His integrity was not just broken; it was shattered. But he thought his good behavior in one part of his life would cover the sin in another part of his life.

Because he was the king, David didn't have to answer to anyone—except to God, who saw everything. *"But the thing David did displeased the Lord,"* the Bible says (2 Samuel 11:27). So God confronted David through a prophet, and David admitted his wrongdoing. He asked God for forgiveness in a moving prayer recorded in Psalm 51. Here we see David's understanding of integrity and where it lies:

Surely you desire truth in the inner parts; you teach me wisdom in the inmost place.

Psalm 51:6

How to Develop and Keep Your Integrity

In these troubled times, the temptation to breach your integrity may be greater than ever before. You will be confronted with making unwise or careless choices that momentarily seem to be a quick fix for a problem you are facing. You may be tempted to "fudge" just a little, to move the numbers around, to give a false impression, or to do something because it makes you feel good. Don't do it. You may fool some people, but you won't fool God. Remember that integrity is complete honesty in every part of your life. It's doing the right thing—all of the time—even when nobody is looking.

Developing and maintaining a life of integrity begins with seeking purity. This doesn't mean you are a "prude" or a goody-two-shoes. Nobody likes someone who flaunts their goodness. But you can be someone with a pure heart. This is the way God wants you to be, and He offers a promise:

"Blessed are the pure in heart, for they will see God."

Matthew 5:8

What a great benefit to living a life of integrity and purity! When you refuse to compromise in the small things as well as the big things in your life, you will have an intimacy with God that is unlike anything you have ever experienced. Isn't that what you need in these troubled times?

A very practical way to keep your heart pure is to form godly habits. What that means is that you routinely do things that please God and give Him glory. Here's what the Bible says:

So whether you eat or drink or whatever you do, do it all for the glory of God.

1 Corinthians 10:31

The way you glorify God is to simply make Him look good. People all around you can't see God, but they can see the evidence of God in your life. When you live a life of integrity, the things you do on the outside that come from a heart of integrity and purity will reflect positively on other people and the way they view God.

Keep God in Your Sights

In order to keep living a life of integrity, you need to keep God in your sights. You need to have a vision that focuses on God and what He wants you to do. Having a vision is like having a goal. It's aspiring to do more than you are doing and to be more than you are.

In these troubled times, it's easy to get bogged down in the cares and concerns of everyday living. Certainly you need to attend to your daily issues, but you also need to have a vision for where you are going. When the storm passes and the dust settles, where do you want to be? What kind of person do you want to be? Keeping God in your sights—having a godly vision—will help you live a life of integrity.

Where there is no vision, the people cast off restraint; but blessed is he who keeps the law.

Proverbs 29:18

As you give God the gift of integrity by living a life of purity, and you keep God in your sights by having a godly vision, something wonderful will happen to you. Even though your outer circumstances may seem difficult, you are going to develop inner peace like you have never known. As a result, you will possess a hope that will fill your life, because your hope will be anchored in God. David understood this. He knew that ultimately his strength and protection was to be found in a life of integrity. May his prayer be your prayer as well:

Guard my life and rescue me; let me not be put to shame, for I take refuge in you. May integrity and uprightness protect me, because my hope is in you.

Psalm 25:20-21

PERSEVERANCE

Consider it pure joy, my brothers, whenever you face trials of many kinds, because you know that the testing of your faith develops perseverance.

James 1:2-3

PERSEVERANCE

One of the most famous speeches in history is Winston Churchill's immortal "Never Give In" speech, which he gave to students at Harrow School in England on October 29, 1941. The war in Europe had been raging for two years, and Britain had just endured eight months of sustained bombing by German aircraft, including 57 consecutive nights of bombing on the city of London.

As Britain's Prime Minister, Winston Churchill found it necessary to bolster the confidence of a battle-weary nation. He knew the war was far from over, and he needed the citizens of England to remain steadfast in spite of overwhelming difficulties, obstacles, discouragement, and fear. Essentially, Churchill needed the people to develop an attitude of perseverance. That's why he gave this impassioned speech:

"Never give in, never give in, never, never, never, never—in nothing, great or small, large or petty—never give in, except to convictions of honor and good sense. Never yield to force; never yield to the apparently overwhelming might of the enemy."

Winston Churchill

Do you ever feel like giving in when faced with overwhelming obstacles or opposition? Everyone does at one time or another. In troubled times, when you face challenges in your life, you need *strength* to stand, *courage* to move forward, and *integrity* to make the right choices. But even with these essential qualities of heart, mind, and character, you may still feel at times like giving in and giving up, something that usually happens when you lose all hope. When that happens—and it will happen—you need perseverance, one of the greatest of all human qualities, and one of hope's most important ingredients.

Stay the Course

There's a reason why perseverance is so important for anyone looking for hope. Simply put, perseverance keeps you going when you feel like giving up. By definition, perseverance is staying the course. It's sticking with something. In the race between the tortoise and the hare, the tortoise represents perseverance; the tortoise wins the race not by being fast and furious, but by being steady, plodding, and persistent.

Perseverance also means that you endure and overcome difficulties, obstacles, discouragement, and fear. The apostle Paul was such a person. Paul was one of the greatest teachers and missionaries the world has ever known. Over a period of 30 years in the middle of the first century, Paul traveled thousands of miles, preached to countless numbers of people, started dozens of churches, and wrote more books in the New Testament than anyone else. With everything Paul did for God and the Gospel, you would think God would have shown favor to Paul by protecting him and making life easy. But that wasn't the case. Read what Paul says about the hardships he endured, and how he persevered:

As servants of God we commend ourselves in every way: in great endurance; in troubles, hardships and distresses; in beatings, imprisonments and riots; in hard work, sleepless nights and hunger...dying, and yet we live on; beaten, and yet not killed; sorrowful, yet always rejoicing; poor, yet making many rich; having nothing, and yet possessing everything.

2 Corinthians 6:4,5;9,10

Keep Going

From Paul's dramatic account, we can learn a lot about perseverance. First of all, you don't have to be perfect to persevere. People often get discouraged and give up because they've made mistakes, or they think they aren't good enough for a particular task, or they are in such a desperate place that they think no amount of perseverance could possibly help. Truth is, you don't persevere when the conditions in your life are perfect. If that were the case, why would you need to persevere? Being in a place or a position where you need to persevere means you are in trouble. It means you are having difficulty. It means you are afraid. And when you are in such a place or position, perseverance is the one thing that will keep you going.

When you get into a frame of mind and heart that says, "*I will persevere*," it means you are realistic about your situation, just like

Paul was realistic about his. Even though you aren't yet where you need or want to be—and you know you have a long journey ahead of you—you don't quit. You press on. You persevere.

Second, perseverance means quitting is not an option. When you quit, it basically means you are giving in and giving up. When you are doing something worthwhile and you know you are doing the right thing, perseverance is the way you finish the task and do what you know is right. Perseverance does not mean you accept the status quo or stay in a rut. When you persevere, you aren't desperately hanging on for dear life, hoping that you don't fail. Perseverance means you are moving forward—even if it's slow and steady—toward a new posture of strength.

Remember the apostle Paul. He was never willing to accept the status quo. He never got stuck in a rut. Paul's perseverance was active and alive, moving him from where he was toward a place of victory and achievement. Notice the dynamics of Paul's persevering personality:

I press on toward the goal to win the prize for which God has called me heavenward in Christ Jesus.

Philippians 3:14

Finally, perseverance is more than self-confidence. As much as perseverance sounds like it's you mustering up the courage and confidence required to stay the course, it's more about finding your confidence in God. There's nothing wrong with self-confidence, but when the difficulties you face are too great, your own confidence will falter. In order to truly experience perseverance, you need to rely on God to see you through. Paul is very clear that your confidence needs to be in God, who has promised to complete the "good work" He began in you:

Being confident of this, that he who began a good work in you will carry it on to completion until the day of Christ Jesus.

Philippians 1:6

The Essence of Perseverance

Perseverance carries with it the idea of endurance, but it is much more. At it's core, perseverance is endurance combined with confidence. Perseverance is believing that what you are looking for is going to happen, not because of your strength and courage, but because of God's. And here's something else about God that should give you confidence: God will never let you down. You may not feel that way at the moment, when you're on the brink of defeat and completely discouraged. But when you persevere and get through your current trials, you will come to the full realization that God has made an unwavering commitment to you. What that means on a practical level is that your endurance will prevail because God will always be with you.

Perseverance is at the heart of hope. Perseverance gets you from your darkest hour to a brighter day. Perseverance is knowing that

God is in your corner, and as a result, choosing to believe there are better days ahead. Once again, read what Paul has to say:

What, then, shall we say in response to this? If God is for us, who can be against us?

Romans 8:31

The Promise of Perseverance
We've uncovered the reasons why perseverance is important. You need it to get you from where you are now to where you need to be. Without perseverance, you would likely give up and miss out on

the benefits and blessings waiting for you on the other side of your trials. That's why Paul encourages us to "hang in there" in another one of his letters:

Let us not become weary in doing good, for at the proper time we will reap a harvest if we do not give up.

Galatians 6:9

Isn't that a great promise? And don't you love the image of the "harvest"? It's the picture of God working together with us to produce something beneficial that comes neither early nor late, but "at the proper time." We may plant the crop, but God makes it grow, and He brings it to fruition in His perfect time. That's what happens when we persevere.

And here's something else that happens when you persevere. Not only will you reap a harvest at the proper time, but you also will be changed into a better person as a result of your perseverance. Nobody likes to go through hard times. It's not something we choose for ourselves. But the truth is that when you do go through difficulties, you grow in profound ways. You get stronger, you gain courage, and you get in the habit of making the right choices. In short, you grow into the kind of person God wants you to be.

This is why the obstacles you are facing now are not random. The trials you are dealing with are not without purpose. God isn't in the business of throwing obstacles in your path, and He doesn't necessarily bring about the trials you are enduring. But He knows about them and He wants very much to help you get through them, if you will ask Him for help and call out, *"Here I am."* Even more, God wants you to develop in mind and character, becoming more and more the person He wants you to be. In fact, you could say that without various difficulties and obstacles, you would not have the opportunity to grow into a wise and spiritually mature person.

We aren't suggesting that you should ask God to give you trials; you likely have more than enough to deal with already! But rather than complaining about your situation, rather than blaming God for the bad things that are happening to you, take on an attitude of thanksgiving and joy for the opportunity that awaits. If you will simply put your trust in God and persevere, He will provide.

Consider it pure joy, my brothers, whenever you face trials of many kinds, because you know that the testing of your faith develops perseverance. Perseverance must finish its work so that you may be mature and complete, not lacking anything.

James 1:2-4

HOPE

...we also rejoice in our sufferings, because we know that suffering produces perseverance; perseverance, character; and character, hope. And hope does not disappoint us...

Romans 5:3-5

HOPE

There's a little verse tucked away in the book of Proverbs in the middle of the Bible that speaks volumes about the human condition. Maybe it describes how you are feeling at this particular time in your life:

Hope deferred makes the heart sick, but a longing fulfilled is a tree of life.

Proverbs 13:12

Hope is a wonderful thing to have. It's the feeling that the events in your life will turn out for the best, even if it doesn't happen exactly the way you envision. When the things you've hoped for don't happen, or the events in your life don't turn out so well, it can literally cause your heart to be sick. But when your dreams and longings are fulfilled, you feel as though your life has tapped into a source of joy that will never end. As the Bible says, you are *"like a tree planted by streams of water"* (Psalm 1:3).

Hope is the theme of this book because hope is something we all need, especially with everything that's going on right now. Whether you've been reading this book in one sitting, or you have digested it in pieces, you have probably been looking forward to this final chapter because you're looking for a reason to hope. It may be that your own hope for a better future has been deferred because of conditions outside your control. Your dreams and aspirations may be on hold. You may even believe they've been shattered with no hope for recovery. If this is the case, you may literally be heartsick right now.

We can't promise that your immediate circumstances are suddenly going to turn around, at least not from a human perspective. But we can offer some words of comfort and encouragement that things will get better, at least from God's perspective. No matter how dark the night may seem, the dawn will come. As sick as your heart may be right now, someday your longing for a brighter future will be fulfilled.

Hope and Waiting

"To be human is to be in trouble," writes Eugene Peterson. It's part of the human condition. You may be someone who's in trouble. You may feel like crying out to God like this writer in the Psalms:

Out of the depths I cry to you, O LORD;
O Lord, hear my voice.   Let your ears
be attentive to my cry for mercy.

Psalm 130:1,2

God hears you when you call out to Him. He knows your troubles, and even more than that, the condition of your heart. If you had your way, God would answer you right now and take away your trouble. But with rare exception, that's not the way God works. He hears your cries for help, and He wants to help you, but He wants to help you in His way and in His time. Right now He wants you to trust Him by waiting and hoping.

I wait for the L{ORD}, my soul waits, and in his word I put my hope. My soul waits for the Lord more than watchmen wait for the morning, more than watchmen wait for the morning.

Psalm 130: 5,6

Notice how the words *wait* and *hope* are linked together, and both words are connected with the image of watchmen waiting for the morning. Here's the thing about watchmen: they can't do a thing to hasten the coming of the dawn, but they know the dawn is coming, and knowing gives them hope. Meanwhile, a watchman doesn't sit back and do nothing. He focuses on what needs to be done and stays alert for potential danger. A watchman knows he has to take the job seriously; he can't do something irresponsible, like falling asleep. In fact, a good watchman will do everything it takes to keep what he's guarding safe and secure. And even though he is alone on his watch, the watchman knows he isn't really alone. If he needs help, he can call on the owner of the property.

In a spiritual sense, being a watchman means acting with strength, courage, integrity and perseverance to focus on the job that needs to be done and to stay alert for potential danger. You take your life seriously, especially when you get into trouble.

You don't have to fear the circumstances around you, because your confidence is in God, trusting Him to do what He said He will do. By waiting on God and putting your hope in Him, you are giving Him time and room to work in your life. You don't have to be heartsick, because you know you can ask God for help, and He will be faithful to answer you. There is a bottom to your trouble, and there will be an end to your night. You are not waiting in vain, but with hope.

Even though you may feel as though you are alone in your trouble, you are not alone. You can call on God, who loves you and cares about you more than you will ever know. When you call, He will answer.

Yet this I call to mind and therefore I have hope: Because of the L<small>ORD</small>'s great love we are not consumed, for his compassions never fail. They are new every morning; great is your faithfulness. I say to myself, "The L<small>ORD</small> is my portion; therefore I will wait for him."

Lamentations 3:21-24

Hope and Faith

Earlier in the book we referred to a verse (2 Chronicles 16:9) in the Bible that says God is looking for those whose hearts are fully committed to Him so that He may "strengthen" them. There's another passage in the Bible that further informs us about the kind of person God is looking for so that He may "deliver" them:

But the eyes of the LORD are on those who fear him, on those whose hope is in his unfailing love, to deliver them from death and keep them alive in famine.

Psalm 33:18,19

Notice how our deliverance is connected to fearing God and putting our hope in God's love. We've talked a lot about fear in this book, but this kind of fear has nothing to do with being afraid of God. We have nothing to fear from God, but we do need to take Him seriously and do what He says. That's what it means to fear God. Taking God seriously is the first step to having true hope and faith in God. You want to do what God says, not because you are forced to, but because you trust God completely and you know He loves you unconditionally.

May your unfailing love rest upon us, O LORD, even as we put our hope in you.

Psalm 33:22

The love of God is the most powerful force in the world. Love defines God's character, and love motivates God to always do what's best for us. We can put our hope in the knowledge that God loves us more than we can even imagine. In fact, He loves us so much that He made the ultimate sacrifice for us so we could be in a relationship with Him. In the most famous verse in the Bible, Jesus tells us what God did out of love for us:

"For God so loved the world that he gave his one and only Son, that whoever believes in him shall not perish but have eternal life."

John 3:16

Believing in God and trusting His plan for us through Jesus is the essence of faith. But it's more than believing that God exists. Most people believe in God, but they don't trust Him. Trusting God means that you literally put your life in His hands, believing that who He is (His character) and what He says in His word (His promises) are not only true, but also true for *you*.

This is what faith in God is all about. It's where your relationship with God begins, when you admit that your own efforts—not just in your current troubling situation, but also in your whole life—aren't enough. When you put your faith in God, you are literally putting your hope in Him and His plan for you through Jesus. You are trusting Him to deliver on His promises and you have confidence that He will, because God is completely reliable and completely trustworthy. This is why you can rejoice in your hope.

Therefore, since we have been justified through faith, we have peace with God through our Lord Jesus Christ, through whom we have gained access by faith into this grace in which we now stand. And we rejoice in the hope of the glory of God.

Romans 5:1,2

Hope and Suffering

As we talk about the kind of hope that is found in the Bible, we have to be aware that suffering is part of the process. We don't like to think about this because we mistakenly think that God's "best" for us means a life free from suffering. But that is not the way it works. The reality is that hope and suffering are linked together.

If this doesn't sound right, consider this: during the first century, when the New Testament was written, most Christians were suffering. They were persecuted for their faith and there was famine in the land, resulting in economic hardships. Yet the Christians were hopeful because they trusted in God. They rejoiced in their suffering, not because they enjoyed difficulty, pain, and sorrow, but because they knew God was using their troubles to build their character. That's why Paul could say that it's possible to rejoice in both your hope and your suffering:

And we rejoice in the hope of the glory of God. Not only so, but we also rejoice in our sufferings, because we know that suffering produces perseverance; perseverance, character; and character, hope. And hope does not disappoint us...

Romans 5:2-5

Like the first-century Christians, you can have hope in the future despite your circumstances if you place your hope in God and trust Him in everything. When you do, you can be confident in this: God will give you *strength* when you are weak; and when you are afraid, God will give you *courage*. In return, when you are faced with difficult choices, you can determine to be a person of *integrity*; and when you feel like giving up, you can choose to have *perseverance*.

While others are reeling and withering from the incredible *change* going on all around them, your *hope*—rooted in your faith and watered by God's love—will allow you to live through difficult circumstances with a peace that passes human understanding (Philippians 4:7). This is the essence of what it means to be a person of faith. This is what it means to have *hope*.

The Hope of Heaven

Do you believe in heaven? Most people do, but only on a *wishing* level. They wish heaven exists, if for no other reason than it suggests a world better than this one. Yes, heaven offers eternal life infinitely better than the temporary life we have now, but we don't have to wish it to be true. You can believe by faith that heaven is a real place. You can legitimately have the hope of heaven and believe that God has prepared it for you, even though you can't see it.

Now faith is being sure of what we hope for and certain of what we do not see.

Hebrews 11:1

If our hope in God was only for this life—the one we live during our time on earth—it would be enough. From God's perspective, however, it's not enough. His plans for us are not limited to our earthly existence. Because God's desire for us is that we live with Him and enjoy Him forever, He has prepared a place for us in heaven.

If you believe God's plan for you through Jesus, you can have real hope that there is a real place called heaven, created by God to last forever. Heaven is where Jesus lives now (Acts 3:21), and where those who trust in Jesus will live in the future (John 14:2). True believers will see Jesus face-to-face in heaven. In fact, believers will be glorified—that is, raised up with Jesus, seated and exalted with Him in heaven (Ephesians 2:6). You won't be sitting on a cloud strumming a harp in heaven. You will worship God and enjoy every blessing imaginable.

"Now the dwelling of God is with men, and he will live with them. They will be his people, and God himself will be with them and be their God. He will wipe every tear from their eyes. There will be no more death or mourning or crying or pain, for the old order of things has passed away."

Revelation 21:3,4

Sharing Your Hope

Believing and understanding that the hope of heaven is real should give you tremendous assurance. But you don't have to wait for heaven to experience "the hope of the glory of God." You can experience hope right now. As you continue to put your hope and faith in God, trusting Him in every detail, your life is going to be filled with stability and confidence despite the difficult change going on all around you. In a word, your life will be characterized by hope.

As you become a person of hope, something is going to happen, something you may not be ready for: people without hope are going to ask you about the hope that you have. But don't just take our word for it. Here's what the apostle Peter wrote to people in the first century who had hope despite their suffering:

Always be prepared to give an answer to everyone who asks you to give the reason for the hope that you have. But do this with gentleness and respect...

1 Peter 3:15

We can almost guarantee that if you have hope in this day and age, people will want to know why, and they're going to ask you about it. So you need to be ready to give them an answer, not in a way that says you're better than they are or that you have it all together, but rather with a gentle heart and respectful words that take their own beliefs and situation into account. If you don't know what to say, ask God for help. He promises to give you the words, and if you let Him, He will use you to share your hope with others, especially those who need to know that God loves them and wants a relationship with them.

This book on hope is coming to an end, but your life of hope is just beginning—if you trust in the God of hope. When you trust God completely, He promises to give you joy and peace in good times and bad, giving you a life overflowing with hope. This is our prayer for you:

May the God of hope fill you with all joy and peace as you trust in him, so that you may overflow with hope by the power of the Holy Spirit.

Romans 15:13

EPILOGUE

We've come to the end of this book of hope, but in many ways this is only the beginning. If you were encouraged as you read this book, and you have a desire to share what you've learned with others, we would like to suggest some ways you can share your hope.

The most direct way you can share hope is to give this book to someone who needs hope. If these words of comfort and encouragement from the Bible have helped you, perhaps they can help someone else—a friend, a member of your family, or someone you happen to meet in the course of your day. Another way is to go online to a special website designed just for you and others who want to share their stories of hope so others can be encouraged:

www.conversantlife.com/hope

A Community of Hope

If ever we needed to come together in a community of hope, the time is now. In fact, such a community already exists, and it's bigger than you think. In every country there are people just like you who have embraced the God of hope. Their relationship with God is real because God is real. As a result, their faith in God has given them assurance for what they hope for and certainty for what they cannot see.

If you have a desire to become part of this dynamic community of hope, we would encourage you to go to www.conversantlife.com/hope to learn more. There you will find information to guide you in your faith journey. And if you have questions, you can ask the community to respond. Most importantly, as you have already discovered in this book, God will respond because, as the Bible says, "he rewards those who earnestly seek him" (Hebrews 11:6).

ADDITIONAL VERSES

VERSES

OF **COMFORT AND ENCOURAGEMENT** FROM THE **BIBLE**

CHANGE

Every good and perfect gift is from above, coming down from the Father of the heavenly lights, who does not change like shifting shadows (James 1:17).

"I the LORD do not change" (Malachi 3:6).

Jesus Christ is the same yesterday and today and forever (Hebrews 13:8).

Heaven and earth will pass away, but my words will never pass away (Mark 13:31).

STRENGTH

The LORD is my light and my salvation—whom shall I fear? The LORD is the stronghold of my life—of whom shall I be afraid? (Psalm 27:1).

The LORD is my strength and my shield; my heart trusts in him, and I am helped. My heart leaps for joy and I will give thanks to him in song (Psalm 28:7).

God is our refuge and strength, an ever-present help in trouble. Therefore we will not fear, though the earth give way and the mountains fall into the heart of the sea though its waters roar and foam and the mountains quake with their surging (Psalm 46:1-3).

Surely the arm of the LORD is not too short to save, nor his ear too dull to hear (Isaiah 59:1).

The Sovereign LORD is my strength; he makes my feet like the feet of a deer, he enables me to go on the heights (Habakkuk 3:19).

Jesus looked at them and said, "With man this is impossible, but with God all things are possible" (Matthew 19:26).

COURAGE

Be strong and take heart, all you who hope in the LORD (Psalm 31:24).

All those gathered here will know that it is not by sword or spear that the LORD saves; for the battle is the LORD's (1 Samuel 17:47).

The LORD is for me, so I will have no fear. What can mere people do to me? (Psalm 118:6).

"I have told you these things, so that in me you may have peace. In this world you will have trouble. But take heart! I have overcome the world" (John 16:33).

For God did not give us a spirit of timidity, but a spirit of power, of love and of self-discipline (2 Timothy 1:7).

Be on guard. Stand firm in the faith. Be courageous. Be strong. And do everything with love (1 Corinthians 16:13,14, NLT).

INTEGRITY

Commit your way to the LORD; trust in him and he will do this: He will make your righteousness shine like the dawn, the justice of your cause like the noonday sun (Psalm 37:5,6).

The integrity of the upright guides them, but the unfaithful are destroyed by their duplicity (Proverbs 11:3).

...the LORD has told you what is good, and this is what he requires of you: to do what is right, to love mercy, and to walk humbly with your God (Micah 6:8, NLT).

"Whoever can be trusted with very little can also be trusted with much, and whoever is dishonest with very little will also be dishonest with much. So if you have not been trustworthy in handling worldly wealth, who will trust you with true riches?" (Luke 16:10,11).

For once you were full of darkness, but now you have light from the Lord. So live as people of light! For this light within you produces only what is good and right and true (Ephesians 5:8,9 NLT).

In everything set them an example by doing what is good. In your teaching show integrity, seriousness and soundness of speech that cannot be condemned...(Titus 2:7,8)

PERSEVERANCE

So, my dear brothers and sisters be strong and immovable. Always work enthusiastically for the Lord, for you know that nothing you do for the Lord is ever useless (1 Corinthians 15:58, NLT).

But you should keep a clear mind in every situation. Don't be afraid of suffering for the Lord. Work at telling others the Good News, and fully carry out the ministry God has given you (2 Timothy 4:5, NLT).

…let us run with perseverance the race marked out for us (Hebrews 12:1).

God blesses those who patiently endure testing and temptation. Afterward they will receive the crown of life that God has promised to those who love him (James 1:12, NLT).

Therefore, prepare your minds for action; be self-controlled; set your hope fully on the grace to be given you when Jesus Christ is revealed (1 Peter 1:13).

Wait for the LORD; be strong and take heart and wait for the LORD (Psalm 27:14).

HOPE

Be strong and take heart, all you who hope in the LORD (Psalm 31:24).

O Lord, you alone are my hope. I've trusted you, O LORD, from childhood (Psalm 71:5, NLT).

But as for me, I will always have hope; I will praise you more and more (Psalm 71:14).

But hope that is seen is no hope at all. Who hopes for what he already has? But if we hope for what we do not yet have, we wait for it patiently (Romans 8:24,25).

For everything that was written in the past was written to teach us, so that through endurance and the encouragement of the Scriptures we might have hope (Romans 15:4).

This is why we work hard and continue to struggle, for our hope is in the living God, who is the Savior of all people and particularly of all believers (1 Timothy 4:10, NLT).

(actual size 1¼")

Medals of Hope

Another way to share the message of hope with those in your life who may be looking for comfort and encouragement is with the "Medals of Hope" pocket reminders. Each medal represents a chapter in this book and is a reminder of what you have read and learned. To share these medals or carry one as a reminder for yourself, go to:

www.bobsiemon.com/hope